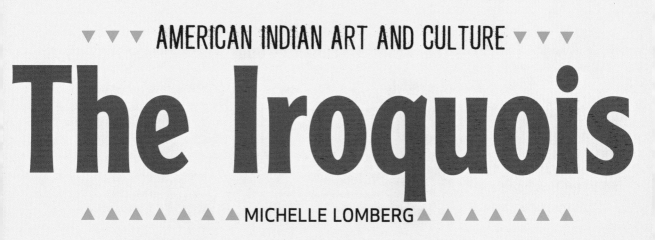

AMERICAN INDIAN ART AND CULTURE

The Iroquois

MICHELLE LOMBERG

www.av2books.com

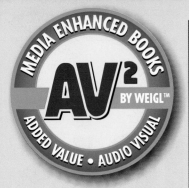

AV² provides enriched content that supplements and complements this book. Weigl's AV² books strive to create inspired learning and engage young minds in a total learning experience.

Your AV² Media Enhanced books come alive with...

Go to **www.av2books.com,** and enter this book's unique code.

BOOK CODE

K 7 5 2 5 8 7

Audio
Listen to sections of the book read aloud.

Key Words
Study vocabulary, and complete a matching word activity.

Video
Watch informative video clips.

Quizzes
Test your knowledge.

Embedded Weblinks
Gain additional information for research.

Slide Show
View images and captions, and prepare a presentation.

AV² by Weigl brings you media enhanced books that support active learning.

Try This!
Complete activities and hands-on experiments.

... and much, much more!

Published by AV² by Weigl
350 5th Avenue, 59th Floor
New York, NY 10118

Websites: www.av2books.com   www.weigl.com

Library of Congress Cataloging-in-Publication Data
Lomberg, Michelle.
 The Iroquois / Michelle Lomberg.
    pages cm. -- (American Indian art and culture)
 Originally published: 2004.
 Includes bibliographical references and index.
 ISBN 978-1-4896-2910-4 (hard cover : alk. paper) -- ISBN 978-1-4896-2911-1 (soft cover : alk. paper) -- ISBN 978-1-4896-2912-8 (single user ebook) -- ISBN 978-1-4896-2913-5 (multi-user ebook)
 1. Iroquois Indians--History--Juvenile literature. 2. Iroquois Indians--Social life and customs--Juvenile literature. I. Title.
 E99.I7L65 2014
 974.7004'9755--dc23
                              2014038976

Printed in the United States of America in Brainerd, Minnesota
1 2 3 4 5 6 7 8 9 18 17 16 15 14

122014
WEP051214

Project Coordinator: Heather Kissock
Art Director: Terry Paulhus

Every reasonable effort has been made to trace ownership and to obtain permission to reprint copyright material. The publishers would be pleased to have any errors or omissions brought to their attention so that they may be corrected in subsequent printings.

Weigl acknowledges Getty Images and Alamy as its primary image suppliers for this title.

Contents

╋ The People

The Iroquois call themselves *Haudenosaunee*, which means "people who live in the extended **longhouse**." This referred to the homes they lived in. Their **Algonquin** enemies gave them the name Iroquois. In Algonquin, the word *Iroquois* means "rattlesnakes." European settlers also used the word Iroquois to refer to this American Indian group.

About 1570, the Mohawk, Oneida, Onondaga, Cayuga, and Seneca nations came together to create one of the world's first **democracies**. This was known as the Iroquois **Confederacy**. Each nation had its own culture, land, and traditions. These different elements were combined to create the Iroquois confederacy.

IROQUOIS MAP

Location of the Iroquois Traditional Lands in New York

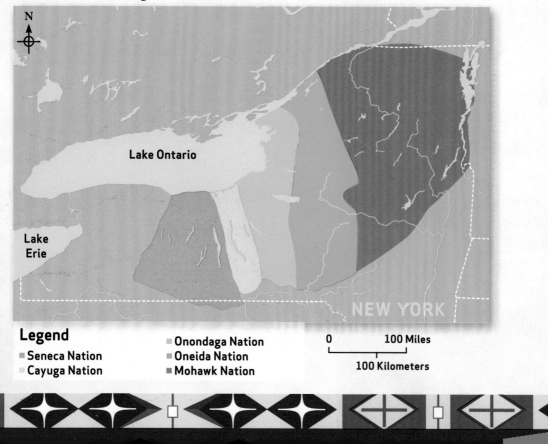

N

Lake Ontario

Lake Erie

NEW YORK

Legend
- Seneca Nation
- Cayuga Nation
- Onondaga Nation
- Oneida Nation
- Mohawk Nation

0   100 Miles

100 Kilometers

The confederacy maintained peace among its members. It also offered each nation help and protection from both warring European settlers and attacks from other American Indian groups.

Iroquois warriors were known for their bravery. Early American settlers learned battle techniques from the Iroquois, which they later used when fighting the British.

NATIONS

The **Seneca** Nation was the **largest** group in the Iroquois Confederacy. The **Oneida** was the **smallest**.

The **Mohawk** had a **tribal council** of men who were chosen by the lead **females** of the group.

The **Onondaga** hosted the annual meeting of the confederacy as their homeland was **in the center of all the nations.**

The **Cayuga** are also known as **the People of the Pipe.** This is because **Chief Big Pipe** was their **leader.**

In **1722**, the **Tuscarora joined the confederacy**. There were now **six nations** belonging to the **Iroquois Confederacy.**

ᛏ Iroquois Homes

The longhouse was the center of Iroquois life. Longhouses were long, narrow buildings with arched roofs. Low porches covered the doorways, which were located at both ends of the longhouse.

To build a longhouse, men tied long wooden poles together to form arches. Then, they placed the poles lengthwise to connect and support the arches. Large shingles made of elm bark covered the whole structure. The Iroquois covered themselves with mats and furs to keep warm. Mats and furs also lined the longhouse walls, providing insulation from the cold.

Longhouses lasted about 20 years before they began to rot.

DWELLING AND DECORATION

The Iroquois built platforms along the interior walls of the longhouse. They used these platforms for sitting and sleeping.

Today, many Iroquois live in framed houses or trailers on **reservation** land. Some Iroquois farm the land, but most land remains in its natural state. Some Iroquois communities have built stores, schools, and banks to house some of the modern services that their residents require.

There was a **10-foot (3-meter) aisle** running through the center of a longhouse.

About **20** families lived in one longhouse.

Longhouses were built from **SAPLINGS** and **TREE BARK.**

The longhouse was divided into **apartments.** Each apartment was **20 feet (6.1 m)** long.

Longhouses were **measured** by their number of **campfires.** A long house might be **10 fires long** or **12 fires long.**

Iroquois Communities

Iroquois villages were organized under a **clan** system. In Iroquois culture, clans were **matrilineal**. Each Iroquois village had a minimum of three clans, which were named after an animal or a bird. Each Iroquois nation had a Turtle, Wolf, and Bear clan.

Each clan had its own longhouse. Families of the same clan lived together in these longhouses. Clan members worked together and shared resources. The oldest woman in a clan was the clan mother. She selected the chief of the clan. Chiefs were always men. The chief represented the clan at village and tribal **councils**. The clan mother also named the children of the clan. This practice continues among many Iroquois families today.

The Iroquois men caught deer to feed their families.

The men in Iroquois communities built the longhouses. They made their own tools for this from stone, bone, and wood. They hunted animals, such as bear and deer. They fought wars and defended their villages from attackers. Women grew and preserved food. They cooked meals and made clothes. They also cared for young children. Both men and women helped make decisions that affected their community.

Children were an important part of Iroquois culture. They were taught the skills they needed to survive as adults from a young age. Grandmothers and grandfathers told stories that taught the Iroquois children values and history. Today, most Iroquois communities have two types of government—elected and traditional.

The Iroquois also use songs and dances to teach history and culture to their children.

People remained members of their clans for their entire lives. Clan members could not marry each other. When a couple married, the husband moved into his wife's longhouse, but he did not become a member of her clan. He remained a member of his mother's clan.

Children belonged to the mother's clan.

Iroquois Clothing

Traditional Iroquois clothing was both useful and beautiful. Iroquois women made clothes from deerskin. They sewed the clothes with bone needles, using **sinew** as thread. They decorated the clothes with porcupine quills and shell beads. Popular beadwork designs included flowers, leaves, and clan symbols. Strawberries were a popular symbol because they were the first fruit to bloom in the new year and they represented a new beginning.

Women wore deerskin dresses, skirts, and leggings. Sometimes, they wore belts or sashes around their waists. Women also wore beautiful beaded headbands.

Men wore leggings and breechcloths to cover their lower bodies.

Iroquois men usually wore fringed deerskin shirts, but in hot weather, they wore deerskin **sashes** instead of shirts. They also made sashes from plant fibers by weaving the fibers together. The leggings and breechcloths worn by men were made of deerskin with fringed edges. Men often wore hats that were decorated with feathers, beads, and porcupine quills.

Both men and women wore deerskin **moccasins**. Iroquois moccasins were cuffed at the ankle. They decorated the cuff and the top of the moccasin with porcupine quills or shell beads.

The Iroquois were known to make shoes from braided cornhusks.

ADORNMENTS

As the Iroquois began to trade with Europeans, they acquired materials such as cloth, glass beads, and ribbon. They incorporated these items into traditional clothing. Today, Iroquois people wear store-bought clothes. However, they still use **calico** to make traditional clothing, such as shirts, dresses, skirts, and sashes. They decorate these items with beads and silver **brooches**.

Colorful beads were sewn onto fabric such as black velvet to make beautiful clothing and bags.

ᛏ Iroquois Food

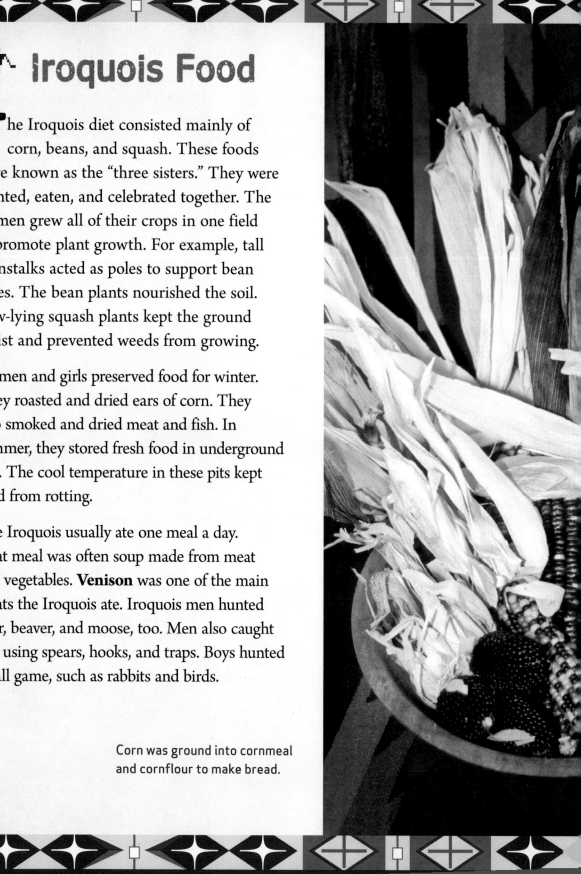

The Iroquois diet consisted mainly of corn, beans, and squash. These foods were known as the "three sisters." They were planted, eaten, and celebrated together. The women grew all of their crops in one field to promote plant growth. For example, tall cornstalks acted as poles to support bean vines. The bean plants nourished the soil. Low-lying squash plants kept the ground moist and prevented weeds from growing.

Women and girls preserved food for winter. They roasted and dried ears of corn. They also smoked and dried meat and fish. In summer, they stored fresh food in underground pits. The cool temperature in these pits kept food from rotting.

The Iroquois usually ate one meal a day. That meal was often soup made from meat and vegetables. **Venison** was one of the main meats the Iroquois ate. Iroquois men hunted bear, beaver, and moose, too. Men also caught fish using spears, hooks, and traps. Boys hunted small game, such as rabbits and birds.

Corn was ground into cornmeal and cornflour to make bread.

Mohawk Corn Bread

Ingredients:

- 1 pound cornflour
- 2 cups canned kidney beans
- salt to taste
- water

Equipment:

- large bowl
- wooden spoon
- large pot
- slotted spoon
- butter knife

Directions:

1. Mix the flour, beans, and salt with some water. Add enough water to create a stiff dough.

2. Mold the dough into round patties. Each patty should be about 6 inches (15.2 centimeters) wide and 2 inches (5 centimeters) thick.

3. With an adult's help, carefully place the patties in boiling water. After about 1 hour, the patties will rise to the top of the water.

4. Ask an adult to help you remove the patties from the water using a slotted spoon. Let the patties cool.

5. Use a butter knife to butter a patty. For a traditional meal, serve the corn bread patties with squash. Corn bread patties can also be served with maple syrup.

Tools, Weapons, and Defense

The Iroquois used tools to hunt and fish. They also used tools to build longhouses and canoes, prepare food, and make clothing. Iroquois building tools included axes, adzes, and chisels. Axe heads were made of stone, which was ground and polished against other stones to make it sharp. The axe head fit inside a wooden handle. An adze was a tool the Iroquois used to chop down trees and shape wood. Adzes also had stone heads and wooden handles. The Iroquois used stone or antler chisels to peel bark from logs, too.

Iroquois war clubs were made of stone and wood.

The Iroquois used canoes for traveling in and for fishing.

Iroquois women used tools to grow and prepare food. They used pointed digging sticks to plant crops. They ground corn using a mortar and pestle. The mortar was made from a length of tree trunk that had a shallow dish carved in the top. The pestle was a heavy, blunt piece of wood.

Iroquois women needed many tools to make clothing. Women used stone and bone scrapers to remove flesh from animal hides. Bone tools called **awls** were used to punch holes for sewing with bone needles.

Bone tools, such as awls and needles, have been discovered at historical Iroquois sites.

HUNTING TOOLS AND WAR WEAPONS

Arrowheads were made of **flint**, a stone that can be **chipped** to form a **sharp point.**

The Iroquois used a variety of **traps** made of **wood, rawhide,** and **sinew** to catch animals, birds, and fish.

Iroquois men hunted **large** and **small game** with bows and arrows.

The **Iroquois** were skilled **woodworkers.** They **steamed wood** so it could be bent into **curved tools.**

The Iroquois began using guns in the **1600s** for **hunting** and **fighting.**

✝ Iroquois Religion

Religion was an important part of traditional Iroquois life. Religious beliefs varied from nation to nation. The Iroquois believed that everything around them had a spirit. These spirits controlled the weather, crops, and animals. Most Iroquois believed in a powerful creator named the Great Spirit. The Iroquois performed several rituals and ceremonies to give thanks to the Great Spirit. The Iroquois believed the Great Spirit had an evil twin brother who caused mischief and suffering.

Medicine and religion were closely tied in Iroquois culture. Medicine societies were groups of people who performed special rituals to heal the sick and bring well-being to the nation. Medicine rituals often involved singing and dancing. During some rituals, the participants wore masks made of wood or cornhusks. The Iroquois believed these masks had great spiritual power.

Medicine dances were sometimes held inside the longhouse.

CREATION

Before the world was created, Sky Man lived on an island in the sky. One day, Sky Man uprooted a tree, leaving a hole in the island. Sky Woman fell through the hole. She fell toward Earth, which was covered with water. As she fell, the animals on Earth tried to save her. To ease her fall, two birds caught Sky Woman on their backs. A frog dove to the bottom of the water to get mud to soften her landing. He placed the mud on a turtle's back.

The frog continued to place mud on the turtle's back. Soon, there was so much mud on the turtle's back that the continent of North America formed. The Iroquois call North America Turtle Island.

One day, Sky Woman gave birth to twin boys. One twin was good, and the other was evil. The good twin was worshipped as the Great Spirit. He created all that is good on Earth. The evil twin created all that is bad.

Ceremonies and Celebrations

The Iroquois often gathered to celebrate and give thanks for the gifts of the Great Spirit. Ceremonies honored different harvests and events throughout the year. One of the many Iroquois celebrations was the Green Corn Festival, which is the oldest Iroquois ceremony. This festival was celebrated every year at the beginning of the corn harvest in August. The Green Corn Festival lasted several days. There were speeches of thanks and offerings of tobacco to the Great Spirit. There were also dances, feasts, and games. The Iroquois celebrated the end of the corn harvest with the Harvest Festival.

The Iroquois would only eat some of the corn at the Green Corn Festival. The rest of the crop would be harvested and dried for winter.

Today, dancing is still an important feature at festival celebrations.

The largest Iroquois celebration was the Midwinter Festival. The six-day festival was celebrated at the beginning of the new year to give thanks to the Creator. People prepared for the festival by cleaning their longhouses. They also talked about their dreams and how those dreams had guided them through the past year. When the festival began, people visited each other's longhouses to stir the fire ashes inside. Stirring the ashes was symbolic of renewal. They scattered the fire of the old year before the new fires were lit. This festival featured feasts, dances, and games.

GAMES

When they were not working or celebrating, the Iroquois enjoyed playing games. They played the bowl game using a bowl filled with six plum or peach stones. The stones were painted black on one side. Players guessed whether the dark or light sides of the stones would face upward when the bowl was banged on the ground.

The Iroquois also enjoyed sports such as lacrosse and stickball, which were similar to what is now known as field hockey. Another popular sport was Snow Snake. In this game, players competed to see who could slide a long stick farthest across the snow.

Lacrosse balls were made from animal skin or wood.

Music and Dance

Iroquois of all ages enjoyed social dances. Some dances were performed by men. Other dances were performed by women. Dancers kept time to a beat played on drums and rattles. The Iroquois made water drums from clay pots that were covered with hide. The drums were filled with water to improve their sound. Rattles were made from bison horns and deer hoofs.

Dancers moved in a counter-clockwise circle, stomping or shuffling their feet. During some dances, dancers challenged each other to dance more quickly as the drumbeat became faster.

The traditional water drum is shaped like a small pot.

CEREMONIAL DANCING

Both men and women performed the round dance. As many as 10 singers sat in the center of a circle. Water drums and rattles accompanied their singing. Women led the dance, and men joined in later. The dancers stepped sideways, one foot at a time. When the rhythm changed, the dancers changed direction.

The Iroquois still enjoy traditional dances. Iroquois and other American Indians host powwows throughout the year. A powwow is a gathering that includes music, dance, food, gifts, and souvenirs.

Powwows are popular events that are attended by many different American Indian groups.

Language and Storytelling

The languages of all six Iroquois nations belong to the Iroquoian language family. These languages are similar, but they are not the same. The Iroquois had no written language. They used images to record history. They wove these images onto beaded belts, called wampum.

Hiawatha was a highly regarded speaker among the Iroquois. He is famous for persuading the Five Nations to join together to form the Iroquois Confederacy.

Iroquoian languages were very expressive. Gifted speakers gained respect for their **wit** and persuasive power. In the Iroquois Confederacy, chiefs of the six nations had to agree **unanimously** on all decisions. Chiefs would make speeches to convince other chiefs to support their decisions.

Storytelling was an important activity in Iroquois culture. When families gathered around longhouse fires, elders told stories. Some stories explained the history of the Iroquois Confederacy. Other stories were about the creation of the natural world.

Today, many Iroquois are trying to preserve their languages. Beginning in the 1800s, the U.S. government sent American Indian children to **boarding schools**. Students learned to speak English at these schools. They were not allowed to speak their own languages. As a result, several generations of Iroquois children did not learn to speak their own language. Today, Iroquois children are no longer sent to boarding schools to learn English. Many Iroquois are learning the Iroquoian languages to preserve this part of their culture.

MONTHS

In the **Mohawk language,** the names of the months reflect the weather and the **agricultural cycle.**

April – Onearahtokha
Fishing Moon

May – Onerahtohko:wa
Planting Moon

June – Ohiariha
Strawberry Moon

July – Onhiarihko:wa
Blueberry (Green Bean) Moon

August – Seskeha
Green Corn Moon

ᛟ Iroquois Art

Traditional Iroquois culture was filled with art. The Iroquois decorated clothing with porcupine quills or shell beads that were beautifully arranged. Striking geometric patterns were woven into baskets. The Iroquois used fine clay pots for storing, cooking, and serving food.

Iroquois women used special techniques to make pots. First, the potter ensured the clay was clean. Then, she added crushed rocks to harden the clay. Iroquois women used their hands and simple tools to shape pots. The pots were dried in the Sun. Once dry, the pots were baked in a fire.

Art also had a spiritual role in Iroquois culture. Men carved elaborate masks for the False Face Society. The False Face Society used masks as part of a ritual to cure illnesses.

Designs were pressed or scratched onto the surface of clay pots while the clay was still damp.

Members of the False Face Society would walk through the woods until they were spoken to by the spirit of a tree. They would then build a fire, sprinkle tobacco, and strip a section of the bark from the tree before carving the mask. Once complete, the mask was cut from the tree.

Masks were considered to be sacred objects.

DRY ART

Today, some Iroquois create art to preserve their culture. They also earn their income by selling their art. Iroquois beadwork has always been admired. Beadworkers have adapted their work over time. Since the 1800s, Iroquois women have beaded souvenir items to sell to tourists. Today, Iroquois beadwork is displayed in galleries and private collections. Iroquois women sell their art at powwows, souvenir shops, and on the Internet.

Some Iroquois earn their income by selling their traditional art.

Wampum

Wampum has a spiritual meaning to the Iroquois. Wampum belts are made by weaving strings of white and purple shell beads into a long strip. The white beads represent peace and harmony. The purple beads symbolize hostility and destruction. The Iroquois used shell beads to create simple shapes. These shapes told stories. Long ago, the Iroquois used wampum belts to record important events or send messages.

Women wove wampum belts by hand and on small **looms**. They strung the beads onto thread made from plant fiber. They wove the threaded beads into long strips of leather or sinew.

Wampum were difficult to make, and this meant the belts were extremely valuable.

Wampum belts had many uses. They were used to invite chiefs to councils. Wampum belts were also traded and given as gifts. A man's family would give a wampum belt to the family of the woman he wanted to marry. If the woman's family accepted the belt, the couple was engaged. The founding of the Iroquois Confederacy is recorded on a wampum belt, too.

Wampum shell beads were used by American Indians as currency for thousands of years.

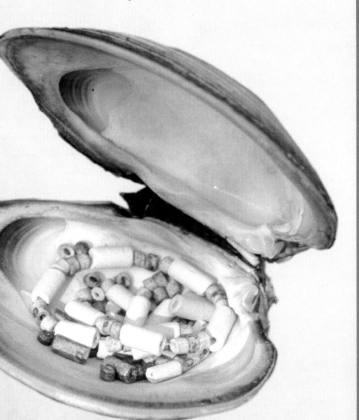

WAMPUM BELTS

Twice a year, **Wampum Keepers** would hold up each belt and **explain** its **meaning** to the people.

Wampum beads are usually **1/4 inch (0.6 cm)** long and **1/8 inch (0.3 cm)** wide.

Beads were used to make **jewelry** such as **necklaces** and **bracelets,** as well as **belts.**

Although **wampum belts** are material objects, their role in the life of the Iroquois was to **make sure promises,** such as elections and choosing officials, were **kept.**

Wampum was used in ceremonies in the **Haudenosaunee** culture to **help heal** families when a family member passed away.

STUDYING THE IROQUOIS' PAST

Archaeologists must search carefully to find traces of Iroquois villages. By carefully searching, archaeologists have found remains of 600-year-old Iroquois villages. Iroquois **artifacts** are some of the hardest to find. Unlike other American Indians, the Iroquois often used materials from plants and animals, which decay over time. Since Iroquois longhouses were made of wood, they would eventually rot away. By looking carefully beneath the surface of the soil, archaeologists can see where a longhouse once stood.

Timeline

Late Woodland Period

B.C.—A.D. **1300**

American Indians in the Upper Great Lakes region began making pottery.

Early Confederacy Period

A.D. **1300—1500s**

Iroquois culture in the New York region began to develop. Iroquois began growing corn, beans, squash, pumpkins, and sunflowers.

Contact Period

A.D. **1300—1500s**

The Iroquois Confederacy was officially founded.

The wooden posts that once supported the longhouse leave round stains in the dirt. These stains are called post molds. Archaeologists can see where apartments and storage areas were located. They can also see where fires were built inside the longhouse. The soil where the hearth was located appears reddish in color. By counting the hearths, archaeologists can estimate how many people lived in the longhouse. Archaeologists also read the writings of Europeans who visited longhouses. Some explorers kept detailed notes about Iroquois life.

By examining post molds, archaeologists can tell the size of a longhouse.

A New Member

1722

The Tuscarora joined the Confederacy and became the sixth member nation.

The War Period

1600s

There were ongoing wars between the Iroquois and the French, who sided with other American Indians such as the Huron.

Modern Period

1600—present

As the traditional way of life declined, many Iroquois settled in urban areas, such as Green Bay, Wisconsin. Many men found jobs in the building industry.

QUIZ

1 Who gave the Iroquois their name?

A. Their Algonquin enemies

2 What does Iroquois mean in the Algonquin language?

A. Rattlesnakes

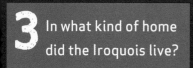

3 In what kind of home did the Iroquois live?

A. A longhouse

4 Which animals were the three main clans of each Iroquois nation named after?

A. Turtle, Wolf, and Bear

5 What did the Iroquois use as thread to sew their clothes?

A. Sinew

6 What did the Iroquois diet mainly consist of?

A. Corn, beans, and squash

7 What is the oldest Iroquois ceremony?

A. The Green Corn Festival

8 What were Iroquois drums made from?

A. Clay pots filled with water

9 Who selected a man to be clan chief?

A. The oldest woma in the clan

10 What color of beads are used to make wampum belts?

A. White and purple

KEY WORDS

Algonquin: an American Indian people who were traditional enemies of the Iroquois, from the Ottawa River area in what is now Canada

archaeologists: scientists who study objects from the past to learn about people who lived long ago

artifacts: objects used or made by humans long ago

awls: sharp tools used for making holes in soft materials

boarding schools: schools where children are sent to live and learn

brooches: large, decorative pins

calico: a heavy, brightly colored cloth

clan: a group of families related to each other

confederacy: a union or alliance of different groups

councils: meetings where people advise on, discuss, or organize something

democracies: governments in which decisions are made by the people or their chosen representatives

longhouse: a long, narrow house made of wood and bark

looms: wooden frames that are used for weaving

matrilineal: kinship that is traced through the mother's lines

moccasins: soft shoes worn by many American Indian groups

reservation: an area of land set aside for American Indians to live on if they choose

sashes: strips of cloth or hide worn over one shoulder and fastened at the waist

sinew: a tough tissue attaching muscle to bone, often used for sewing

unanimously: with everyone agreeing

venison: deer meat

wit: a natural skill in using words and ideas to create humor

INDEX

Log on to www.av2books.com

AV² by Weigl brings you media enhanced books that support active learning. Go to www.av2books.com, and enter the special code found on page 2 of this book. You will gain access to enriched and enhanced content that supplements and complements this book. Content includes video, audio, weblinks, quizzes, a slide show, and activities.

AV² Online Navigation

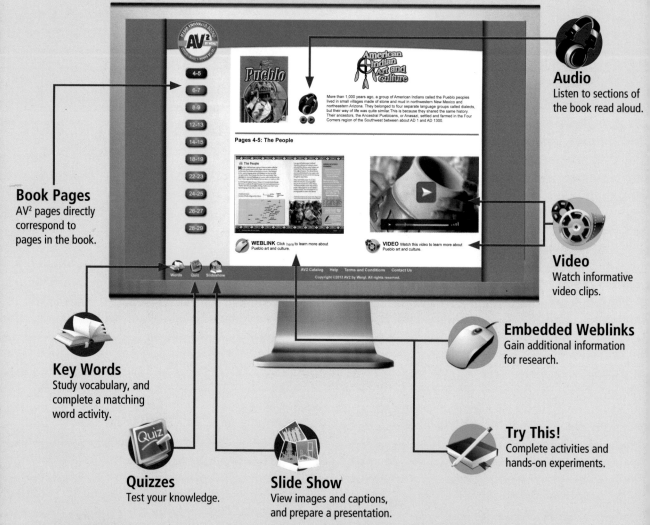

Book Pages
AV² pages directly correspond to pages in the book.

Audio
Listen to sections of the book read aloud.

Video
Watch informative video clips.

Key Words
Study vocabulary, and complete a matching word activity.

Embedded Weblinks
Gain additional information for research.

Quizzes
Test your knowledge.

Slide Show
View images and captions, and prepare a presentation.

Try This!
Complete activities and hands-on experiments.

AV² was built to bridge the gap between print and digital. We encourage you to tell us what you like and what you want to see in the future.

Sign up to be an AV² Ambassador at www.av2books.com/ambassador.